ZENDAYA

by
Emily Klein

SCHOLASTIC INC.

© 2014 by Scholastic
ISBN 978-0-545-67507-9

Published by Scholastic Inc.
SCHOLASTIC and associated logos are trademarks and/or
registered trademarks of Scholastic Inc.

12 11 10 9 8 7 6 5 4 3 2 1   14 15 16 17 18 19/0

Printed in the U.S.A.   40

First printing, January 2014

Table of Contents

INTRODUCTION

Have you ever dreamed of starring in a hit TV show . . . with your BFF? How about singing and dancing in front of huge cheering crowds at your very own concerts? Maybe your dream is to model the hottest fashions. Or write a book filled with brilliant advice. Zendaya Coleman had these dreams, too. And now she's living them.

For three seasons, Zendaya lit up millions of TVs each week with her best friend, actress Bella Thorne, on their hit Disney Channel show *Shake It Up*. She also twirled her way into viewers' hearts on season 16 of *Dancing with the Stars*. Fashionistas scour magazines just to see her latest ensembles. And Zendaya just published a book, *Between U and Me*, and rocked the air waves with her first solo album, *Zendaya*. Even though she's still a teenager, Zendaya is perched on the brink of superstardom. None of her success came easy, though. Zendaya had to work hard and make many sacrifices to make her dreams come true.

CHAPTER 1

Theater Girl

Zendaya—which means "to give thanks" in the Zimbabwean language Shona—was born on September 1, 1996. She grew up in Oakland, California, with her parents, Claire and Kazembe.

When Zendaya was younger, she spent a lot of time at the California Shakespeare Theater. Her mom was the house manager, and Zendaya would tag along to help her mother at work. She also got to watch the actors and actresses on stage.

Even though Zendaya loved to dance and sing at home, she never performed in front of anyone. In fact, she was very shy.

But eventually she realized she wanted to be on that stage, too. "While I spent all that time at the theater with my mom, I fell in love with it . . . I realized that is what I wanted to do," she told *LàTeen*.

Once Zendaya made that decision, there was no stopping her. She studied at several well-known acting schools and became a member of the hip-hop dance troupe Future Shock Oakland. She even learned how to hula dance! All of Zendaya's hard work paid off. She performed on stages all over the world and modeled for companies like Macy's and Old Navy. One time, Zendaya even got to work with Selena Gomez! She was one of her backup dancers in a Sears commercial.

Zendaya loved being on stage. "As soon as I started performing on stage,"

Zendaya explained on *Dancing with the Stars*, "I felt some kind of magical feeling. I couldn't imagine myself doing anything else with my life."

CHAPTER 2

Shaking It Up!

Zendaya's parents have always supported her career. In the beginning, her mom would drive her to auditions and callbacks in the Oakland area. But there wasn't much acting work around there, so Zendaya's dad quit his job to take her to auditions in Los Angeles. When Zendaya auditioned for *Shake It Up*, she thought she would be trying out for the role of CeCe Jones. But she quickly found out casting wanted her to read for the other lead role . . . Raquel "Rocky" Blue.

Zendaya handled the change like a pro. "I really felt Rocky," Zendaya explained to *J-14*. "I had a connection with her character." Zendaya nailed the reading and got the role! Disney exec Judy Taylor told *Variety*, "Zendaya has such a great presence. She's smart, confident, and completely engaging. She's somebody you never tire of watching."

Shortly after she landed the role of Rocky on *Shake It Up*, Zendaya and her dad moved to Los Angeles. Unfortunately, her mom had to stay back in Oakland for a while. "Dads are cool, but dads aren't moms," Zendaya admitted on *Dancing with the Stars* about this time in her life. She loves her dad and was super-excited to be on a TV show, but Zendaya missed having someone she could talk to about "girl stuff." So Zendaya was thrilled when her mom finally joined her in Los Angeles.

Shake It Up debuted in November of 2010. Millions of viewers tuned in to watch Zendaya and Bella play two young dancers who perform on a local dance program called *Shake It Up, Chicago!* Fans loved the show and it quickly raced up the ratings to number one. Zendaya was a star!

Zendaya and her dad.

In addition to *Shake It Up*, Zendaya also got to work on other cool projects. She sang on the three *Shake It Up* albums and shot videos for several of the songs.

"Contagious Love," "Fashion Is My Kryptonite," and "Watch Me" are just a few of those hits. Zendaya was also the voice of Fern in the Disney movie *Pixie Hollow Games*. And she appeared on the Disney shows *Good Luck Charlie*, *A.N.T. Farm*, and *Prank Stars*. Zendaya also played one of the lead roles along with Bella Thorne in the Disney movie *Frenemies*. What was it like filming a whole movie with her bestie? "It makes [filming] ten times more fun," Zendaya told TVGuide.com.

CHAPTER 3

Famous Friends

$\mathcal{S}$hake It Up not only made Zendaya a star, the show also introduced her to her best friend, Bella Thorne. Zendaya told

Seventeen magazine, "Bella and I have rings that say 'sisters.' . . . It's a reminder that I'm never alone." In a different interview, Zendaya told *Seventeen*: "She's very bubbly and bright and I'm more mellow, so we are kind of like our characters in a sense. We fit together so well because whatever I lack she has and whatever she lacks I have."

Zendaya gets to meet and hang out with other celebs, too. She told *MTV News* about the time she met Demi Lovato: "She was very supportive of me and she wanted to know if there is anything that I needed or if I needed someone to talk to, because she definitely went through what I'm dealing with." And in an *M Magazine* video interview, Zendaya told viewers, "I actually got to have dinner with Raven-Symoné and now she's like a mentor and a

big sister to me. . . . She basically told me to have fun, try new things, put myself out there, and to enjoy what I'm doing." Zendaya is also good friends with actor, singer, and dancer Trevor Jackson and got to star in his video "Like We Grown."

CHAPTER 4
Star-Studded Dancing

When she was just sixteen years old, Zendaya signed on to compete on season 16 of *Dancing with the Stars*. She became the youngest contestant ever on the show. She told *Access Hollywood*, "I just want to try new things and put myself out there."

On one episode, Zendaya's *Shake It Up* castmate and former *Dancing with the Stars* contestant Roshon Fegan told viewers, "Zendaya's showing that it doesn't matter how old you are . . . As

long as you believe in yourself and you commit to what you're doing, nothing can stop you."

Even though Zendaya was an awesome dancer, she was used to hip-hop dancing. Hip-hop is very different from the ballroom dancing on *Dancing with the Stars*. "It's basically doing the exact opposite of what I'm used to," she explained on *Good Morning America*. "Not only am I learning something from the beginning, but I also

have to forget what I already know."
During that same interview, Zendaya's
partner, Val Chmerkovskiy, said, "My
partner, Zendaya, is amazing. She's an
incredible student, really talented, great
energy, great focus, and she's doing
amazing."

Zendaya worked hard to learn new
dances like the samba, the quickstep, the

foxtrot, and the salsa. Having to
perfect a new dance style, learn fresh
choreography, and perform live each
week was stressful. But Zendaya gave
her all in every performance and wowed
the judges and viewers. Zendaya and
Val even earned the first perfect score
of the season! Judge Bruno Tonioli told
her, "For somebody so young, you have
pitch-perfect performer instinct."

Week after week, Zendaya won over more and more fans. The duo danced all the way into the finals.

Then, during the dress rehearsal right before the finale, Zendaya and Val had a mishap that almost kept them from competing. Zendaya accidentally elbowed Val above his eye. He started bleeding and couldn't get it to stop. Val told *People* magazine, "If I was going to have to go get stitches, then I wouldn't have time to make it back." Luckily, Val was able to patch up his eye enough to perform. The two sparkled on the dance floor that night and earned several perfect scores. In the end, though, Zendaya and Val came in second place to country music artist and *American Idol* contestant Kellie Pickler.

Zendaya has no regrets about her time on the show. She developed a close bond with Val and also views several of her castmates as protective big brothers. She also told *MTV News*, "I was happy that I made it that far and I think that's the most important thing to take with me."

Throughout the competition, Zendaya

blogged about her experiences on AccessHollywood.com. Shortly after the season ended she wrote, "My dreams are coming true right before my eyes and *Dancing with the Stars* has helped me to realize that I have a lot more to achieve and that I can do anything I put my mind to."

CHAPTER 5
Zswaggers

Zendaya's beloved fans are known as Zswaggers. She says on Zendaya.com, "I created this website to share with all of u what's going on in my world. My Zswaggers mean everything to me! I love you all!!"

Shortly after *Dancing with the Stars*, Zendaya wrote on her *Access Hollywood* blog: "Throughout this process my fans have been beside me the entire way . . . Whenever I would feel down or stressed-out about the competition, I could just scroll through my Twitter mentions and read the wonderful things that my fans would say."

Zendaya knows that her younger Zswaggers look up to her, and she takes that role seriously. While on *Dancing with the Stars*, she passed on the spray tan and refused to wear skimpy costumes.

She also had a message for the Zswaggers who were heartbroken when she didn't win. "I want my young fans to know it's not always about winning the big trophy," she explained in a *HuffPost Live* interview.

"I learned so much and I gained a big brother out of the experience." What's her biggest piece of advice? "Don't forget to smile," she said in the *HuffPost Live* interview. Zendaya often posts "DFTS" on her website with a smiley face.

As much as Zendaya loves her Zswaggers, they are just as protective of her. *J-14* reported that Zswaggers started picking online fights with people who were posting mean messages about Zendaya. This made Zendaya sad. She sent out several tweets reminding her fans to stay positive. Negativity just isn't what this star is about.

CHAPTER 6

Moving On

Although *Shake It Up* was a huge fan fave, Disney decided that season 3 would be its last. Zendaya didn't let this news get her down, though. She told *HuffPost Live*, "Nothing lasts forever, which is why you have to continue to invent yourself and do new things."

And that's exactly what she is doing. Zendaya's schedule is already packed with exciting new projects! She will be starring in the Disney Channel movie

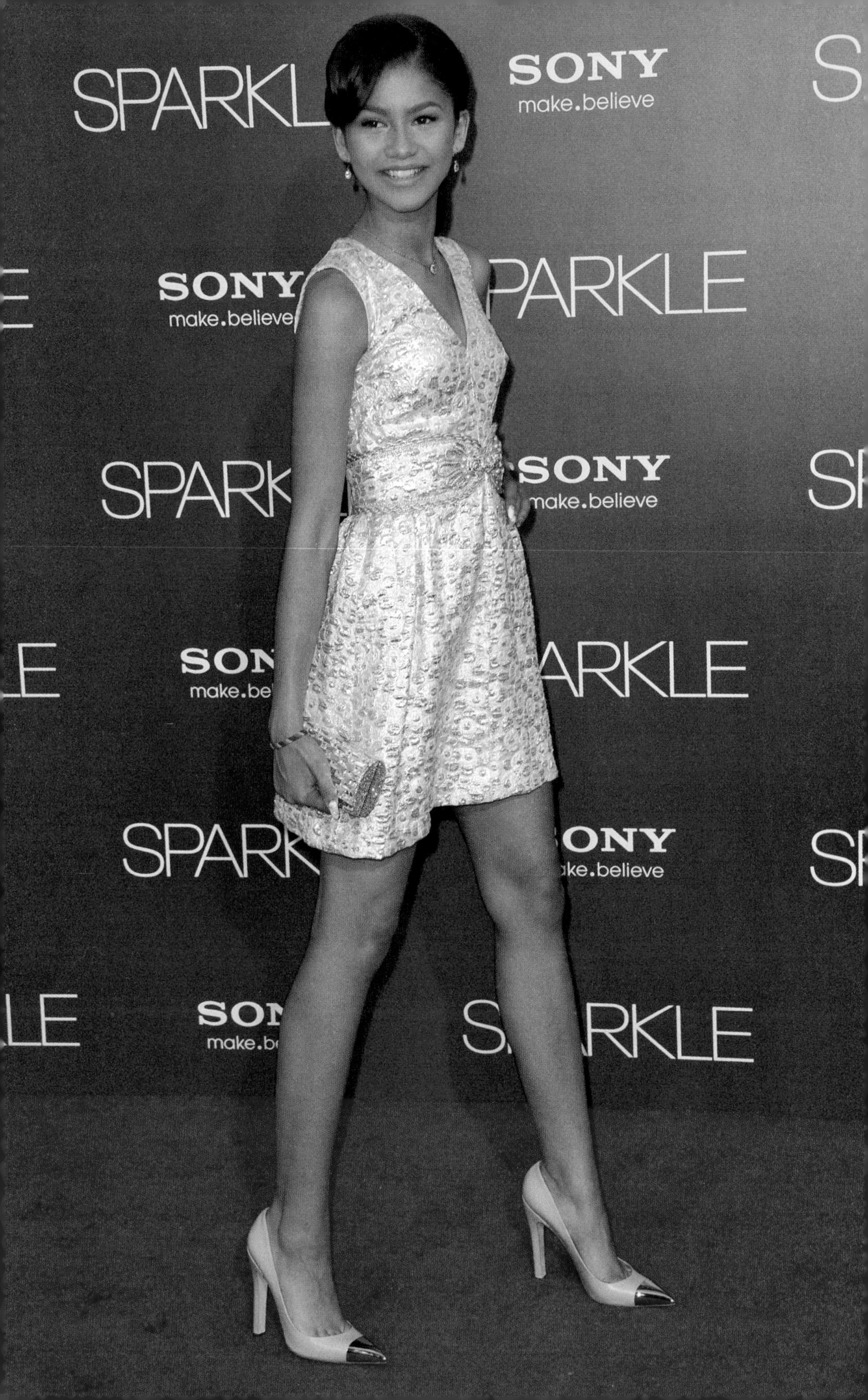
SONY
make.believe

called *Zapped*, based on the book *Boys Are Dogs*. Zendaya also co-wrote an advice book called *Between U and Me: How to Rock Your Tween Years with Style and Confidence*. "I wanted to make something that was actually going to be useful," Zendaya told *MTV News*.

Having just gone through her tween years, Zendaya believes her advice is especially relevant to kids in that age group. Zendaya has also teamed up with the NFL to launch a new line of active wear for teens and juniors. "It reflects my style . . . I have both a [girlie and tomboy look] — and that's what this combines," Zendaya told *Twist*.

Like Hilary Duff and Demi Lovato before her, Zendaya acknowledges her move away from a Disney all-star toward new ventures. "Everyone has done it

differently, and my main thing is that
I don't want people to compare me,"
Zendaya told *MTV News*. She added,
"I'm gonna grow up like Zendaya would
grow up. Who knows how that's gonna
happen, but I think it's going to be pretty
great because I have great parents."

CHAPTER 7

Making Music

Although Zendaya is working on several projects, music is her next career focus. She signed a deal with

Hollywood Records and has already released her first solo album, *Zendaya*. (Zswaggers went crazy over her first single, "Replay".) As she explained to *WSJ Live*, "This is my career. And of course everyone has their input and their ideas, but at the end of the day I have to do what makes me happy and what I truly feel is right."

Zendaya worked with some of the best writers and producers in the industry to help create her vision. "I'm very hands-on. I want to make sure things are perfect," Zendaya told *MTV News*. She also admitted to listening to her songs over and over again until they were exactly what she wanted. She describes this album as rhythmic pop, but admitted that she would like to venture into hip-hop. So, who would Zendaya love to work with? Rap artists A$AP Rocky,

Big Sean, and Kendrick Lamar top her dream list.

Zendaya didn't take control of just the sound of her music. She had input on her "Replay" video and her tour as well. According to Zendaya.com, she worked with music video director Colin Tilley— who has also worked with Justin Timberlake— and hip-hop choreographer Ian Eastwood on the video. She told *WSJ Live*, "I had this whole vision for how I wanted [the single] to be and how I wanted [the video] to look." Zendaya also knew she wanted to tour across the United States with a band made up of other young performers. "I feel it is very important for young people to see other young people on stage," she told *WSJ Live*. She was happy to tell *Fox & Friends* viewers, "I have an eleven-year-old bass player."

Zendaya is always super-busy, but she makes time to perform at special events. She sang the National Anthem before a baseball game at Dodgers Stadium and has even performed at the White House!

CHAPTER 8

Behind the Curtain!

Zendaya loves her exciting new career, but school is also very important to her. "School comes first. Then work [which] I've made a part of my life and it's also what I love to do; and I realize I'm still a kid and still need my time to do regular teenage stuff," she explained to *Kontrol* magazine. Like many child stars, Zendaya is homeschooled and has a teacher who works with her on set. Her favorite subject is science, and

she thinks she may want to be a science teacher one day.

Zendaya also likes to give back to her community. She has donated her time to charities like the Toys for Tots Foundation, and Give Kids the World Village. What is Zendaya's advice for other kids who want to do volunteer work? She told *Hollywood Teen'Zine*, "Start small and then go bigger. Start with a bake sale and give the money to a local charity . . . then work your way up."

Even though Zendaya describes herself as a tomboy, she's also really into fashion. Zendaya likes to experiment with different looks. She rocked a sleek short suit to the Radio Disney Music Awards and donned a dainty pink dress to her friend Bella Thorne's Quinceañera (her fifteenth birthday party). Zendaya also loves wearing high heels—even though she's already five feet ten inches tall! She completes her looks with her signature long nails, which she often decks out in fancy, fabulous designs.

While Zendaya lives the hectic life of a superstar, she does realize her life

is very different from most kids her age. "This is not the normal teenage situation," Zendaya told *MTV News*. "If I were a normal kid, I'd be at school right now." Still, Zendaya does make time for hanging out with friends and video chatting. Zendaya is also really close with her parents. They are her heroes

and her support system. And she loves her giant black schnauzer, Midnight.

Between modeling, acting, singing, and dancing, Zendaya's talents are limitless. What's next for this rising superstar? Lots! She would love to try acting in more dramatic roles and other movies. As she told viewers on *Dancing with the Stars*, "I just wanna continue on this upward spiral to my dreams."

JUST THE FACTS

NAME: Zendaya (pronounced zen-DAY-a) Coleman

BIRTHDAY: September 1, 1996

CURRENT RESIDENCE: Los Angeles, CA

PARENTS: Kazembe Ajamu Coleman and Claire Stoermer

NICKNAME: Z

HEIGHT: 5'10"

PARENTS' HEIGHTS: Mom 6'4", Dad 6'2"

FAVORITE SINGERS: Michael Jackson and Beyoncé

FAVORITE DISNEY STAR: China Anne McClain

FAVORITE MOVIE: *White Chicks*

FAVORITE PLACE TO SHOP: Aritzia

FAVORITE FASHION ITEM: boots

FAVORITE ACTOR: Johnny Depp

FAVORITE SUBJECT: science

FAVORITE STAR AS A CHILD: Raven-Symoné

STAR SHE WOULD LOVE TO INTERVIEW: Beyoncé

OFFICIAL FACEBOOK: facebook.com/Zendaya

OFFICIAL TWITTER: @Zendaya

OFFICIAL SITE: Zendaya.com